DELANEY
STREET
PRESS

A Time to Grieve...

A Time to Heal

A Time to Grieve...

A Time to Heal

A Treasury of Inspiration
And Healing

by Criswell Freeman

DELANEY STREET PRESS
Nashville, TN

ISBN 1-58334-077-7

The ideas expressed in this book are not, in all cases, exact quotations, as some have been edited for clarity and brevity. In all cases, the author has attempted to maintain the speaker's original intent. In some cases, material for this book was obtained from secondary sources, primarily print media. While every effort was made to ensure the accuracy of these sources, the accuracy cannot be guaranteed. For additions, deletions, corrections or clarifications in future editions of this text, please write DELANEY STREET PRESS.

Printed in the United States of America
Cover Design by Bart Dawson
Typesetting & Page Layout by Sue Gerdes

2 3 4 5 6 7 8 9 10 • 05 06 07 08 09 10

ACKNOWLEDGMENTS

The author gratefully acknowledges the helpful support of Angela Beasley Freeman, Dick and Mary Freeman, Mary Susan Freeman, Jim Gallery, and the entire team of professionals at DELANEY STREET PRESS and WALNUT GROVE PRESS.

For Those Who Mourn

Table of Contents

Introduction 15

Part I: A Time to Grieve 17

    Chapter 1: Shock 19

    Chapter 2: Grief Is... 23

    Chapter 3: Expressing Grief 31

    Chapter 4: Unexpected Emotions 41

Part II: A Time to Heal 53

    Chapter 5: Grief's Timetable 55

    Chapter 6: Healthy Grieving 71

    Chapter 7: Living Again 87

Appendix 109

Sources 119

Grief should be the
Instructor of the wise.
Sorrow is knowledge:
They who know the
most must mourn
the deepest.

Lord Byron

Introduction

The quotations on these pages will inform and comfort those who have experienced any significant loss. Through the words of knowledgeable men and women, many of whom are experts in the field of grief counseling, this text explores the roller-coaster emotions of life-changing grief and the healing that inevitably comes with time.

If you are grieving, then you understand all too well the words of the Roman philosopher Publilius Syrus who wrote, "Pain of mind is worse than pain of body." Experience teaches us that the pain of grief attacks every aspect of life. If you are gripped by sorrow, you may feel confused, despondent, or depressed. You may cry constantly or you may be unable to shed a tear. You may feel numb or you may feel searing emotional pain. Whatever your circumstances, this book is intended to help.

As a member-in-good-standing of the human community, you will, during your life, experience the kinds of traumatic loss that result in intense grief. But just as grief is inevitable, so is the healing that comes to those who courageously face their suffering and choose to live again.

Part I
A Time to Grieve

1

Shock

When we receive word of any significant loss, the initial reaction is shock: We simply can't believe what has happened. Even when that loss is expected, grief arrives amid a cloud of numbness.

A brief period of emotional numbness serves an important purpose: It provides us time to absorb the full impact of our loss. Eventually, of course, shock and denial must give way to emotional pain.

If you've recently lost a loved one — or encountered some other significant loss — you may feel intense shock that borders on disbelief. This feeling is normal, as the following quotations attest.

There is little question that the first
reaction to a major loss is shock.
Catherine M. Sanders

The stage of shock and numbness is
so common that it is predictable. It may
be Nature's cloak of protection.
Genevieve Davis Ginsburg

I felt nothing. It was almost as if I'd
been replaced by a robot that had
programmed me to cope.
Dr. Joyce Brothers

When the full impact of our loss hit
home, it seemed that everything
moved in slow motion.

Zig Ziglar

Denial is a natural process our minds
put us through when we need extra time
to process some new and unanticipated
development.

Charlie Walton

Many bereaved people, particularly
in the early days of their grief, are
worried about their lingering
confused state of mind.

Catherine M. Sanders

Another sensation you may experience
is this: almost no feeling at all.
You may feel empty and numb.
That's a common reaction at first.
James E. Miller

Do not be afraid of the shock. That
often comes with the early stages of grief.
Granger Westberg

The shock phase, for all its confusion,
helps us adapt by forming an insulation
against the chaotic outside world.
Catherine M. Sanders

2

Grief Is...

In 1804, Noah Webster defined grief as "the pain of mind, produced by loss, misfortune, injury, or evils of any kind." Nothing has changed since then. When your loss is a profound one, the resulting "pain of mind" can leave you emotionally spent.

Grief is a universal human experience that is nevertheless different for every individual. On the following pages, knowledgeable men and women describe the grieving process. These observations may help you understand the nature of your own feelings.

Grief is the aftermath of any deeply
significant loss.

Wayne Oates

Grief is to man as certain as the grave.

George Crabbe

Grief is a journey, a pilgrimage
something we pass through.

James W. Moore

Loss is a fact of being alive in a mortal,
imperfect world.

Bob Deits

Grief is a natural part
of human experience.

Granger Westberg

Because it is inevitable, it is important
to know that "grief" is not a bad word.

Bob Deits

Grief is always more than sorrow.
It is a rawness you feel at
the center of your being.
Harriet Sarnoff Schiff

Grief affects us spiritually, physically,
socially, and in every other
facet of life.
Zig Ziglar

Grief assaults us physically,
emotionally, mentally, spiritually,
and socially.
Kathlyn S. Baldwin

Grief is preoccupying and depleting.
Judy Tatelbaum

Grief is exhausting.
Catherine M. Sanders

God whispers to us in our pleasures,
speaks in our conscience,
but shouts in our pain.
C. S. Lewis

Sometimes it makes perfect sense
to act a little crazy.
James E. Miller

I didn't have any normal minutes
during those two years. It wasn't just
grief, it was total confusion.
Helen Hayes

You're not going crazy.
You are grieving.

Charlie Walton

Joy has its friends,
       but grief its loneliness.
Robert Nathan

It is such a secret place,
       the land of tears.
Antoine de Saint-Exupéry

If you are caught up in the emotions
  of grief, I don't have to tell you what
they are like; they are all-consuming.
Helen Fitzgerald

3

Expressing Grief

Grief seeks to express itself. When we allow ourselves to honestly express feelings of loss, we are doing the hard work of grieving. When we suppress those emotions, we needlessly prolong the pain.

If you have faced a significant loss, recognize the need to express your grief to others and to yourself. Acknowledge your suffering; mourn your loss; allow the tears to flow. Genuine expressions of grief are not only appropriate, they are also healing. And the sooner you acknowledge your suffering, the sooner that healing begins.

We need to allow ourselves
to experience and express the
sadness, anger, guilt, confusion,
emptiness, and despair that may
be so intense that we may feel
as if we're going crazy.
Kathlyn S. Baldwin

Tears are the natural form of release
for the still-suppressed feelings of
love and gratitude, and also for the
reservoir of pain and sorrow we have
in our hearts.
Zig Ziglar

Giving yourself permission to grieve is a great gift.

Bob Deits

Weeping is only a stage — it won't
last forever so you needn't be
afraid to cry.

Alla Renée Bozarth

There is certain joy in weeping
for by tears, grief is relieved.

Ovid

Let yourself yield to the expressive
emotion in the moment.

Alla Renée Bozarth

Tears are as natural as laughter
and just as healing.
Kathlyn S. Baldwin

Tears are the silent language of grief.
Voltaire

To weep is to make less
the depth of grief.
William Shakespeare

Most mourners report that from time
to time they have wondered whether it is
worth it to adapt or readjust to their loss.
Glen W. Davidson

Sorrow is what we feel. It is that inner
sadness we carry with us as we go
about our daily lives.
Harriet Sarnoff Schiff

Tears from the depths of some divine
despair rise in the heart and gather
to the eyes.
Alfred, Lord Tennyson

If your major symptoms are physical,
consult your primary physician. If your
major symptoms are emotional, consult a
therapist, counselor, or pastor.
Glen W. Davidson

Your feelings may spill forth at times
when there seems to be no outside source
to provoke such a reaction.
Carol Staudacher

Teach your friends not to be afraid
if you are weeping. The tears are merely
emotion turned liquid.
Harriet Sarnoff Schiff

If you find yourself focusing consistently
on self-destructive thoughts,
seek professional help.
Glen W. Davidson

Expressing a wide spectrum of emotions
is healthier than trying to express
no emotion.
Glen W. Davidson

People who try to ignore the powerful
deep-seated emotions of grief usually
see them reappear later.
Helen Fitzgerald

He that conceals his grief
    finds no remedy for it.
Turkish Proverb

The denial of expression of emotion
    does not necessarily destroy
      or dissipate it.
Stanley P. Cornils

Your body has its own healing wisdom
   within it — and so does your soul.
Alla Renée Bozarth

Perhaps in grieving it is more important than in any other endeavor to internalize the saying, "If at first you don't succeed, try, try again."

Harriet Sarnoff Schiff

4

Unexpected Emotions

In times of loss, we expect to feel intense sadness. But we may be surprised and confused by other, unexpected emotions: feelings of anger, guilt, fear, and jealousy. These feelings are normal.

Our anger may be directed at any number of targets: medical staff, friends, family members, or even the deceased. Anger is often accompanied by feelings of guilt. As survivors, we may feel guilty, telling ourselves that we could have done more. Furthermore, we may be jealous of those who have escaped our particular sorrow. And we may be fearful of an uncertain future.

Unexpected emotions are a natural part of the grieving process. Recognizing these emotions — and working through them — is an important step in the journey toward healing.

As their stunned feelings pass,
mourners need to express conflicting
and competing emotions: the need
to cry, to be angry, to laugh and joke
without feeling ostracized.
Glen W. Davidson

Anger is a natural part of grief,
a constant companion of frustration,
helplessness, and deprivation.
Catherine M. Sanders

Anger is attached to grieving.
Don't bury it in "only good and
positive" thoughts.
Genevieve Davis Ginsburg

Anger at the time of death is often
misdirected at family, friends,
or colleagues.
Helen Fitzgerald

You may even be angry with your loved
one who has died. Widows and widowers
frequently feel they have been deserted.
Carol Staudacher

Perhaps one of the easiest things to
forget when a husband or wife has died
is that there is anger in all loving
relationships. Many mourners find
themselves perplexed by this.
Harriet Sarnoff Schiff

Anger, and an accompanying impulse
to place blame on others, is a common
feeling during the grieving process.
Judy Tatelbaum

No matter how often I read and heard
that anger is a stage of grief, I was sure
that would never happen to me.
Genevieve Davis Ginsburg

If your loved one is dead, ask yourself
this question: Are you still
angry at him?
Wayne Oates

Be as angry as you
have to be until the day
comes when your
compassion exceeds
your rage.

Ellen Sue Stern

The feeling of abandonment is one of the most agonizing feelings we must endure and conquer in grief.

Judy Tatelbaum

No one ever told me that grief felt so much like fear.

C. S. Lewis

Talk about your feelings of guilt with someone you trust. Chances are, what you feel guilty about will have been experienced by others.

Catherine M. Sanders

When we imagine that if we had acted differently we might have prevented the death, we figuratively endow ourselves with superhuman powers to change destiny.

Judy Tatelbaum

Take your burdens of guilt to God and leave them with God.

Wayne Oates

Be done with self-blame and get on with life.

Wayne Oates

Jealousy is almost an inevitable part
of being hurt by life. How can the
injured person not feel jealous of
people who have received better?
Harold S. Kushner

You may feel guilty when you begin
to enjoy life again.
Bob Deits

The missing link in finishing with grief
is often forgiveness.
Judy Tatelbaum

If you have experienced grief, there is someone you need to forgive.

Bob Deits

Feel your feelings. They will not destroy you.

Alla Renée Bozarth

Part II
A Time to Heal

5

Grief's Timetable

Once the intense pain of grieving begins, almost everyone asks the same question: "How long will it last?" There is no simple answer to this question. Everyone must grieve in his or her own way and at his or her own pace.

Mourning is a process that cannot be hurried; each significant loss is experienced and processed according to its own timetable. But in the dark night of your own particular grief, it is imperative to remember that healing, like grief, has *its* own timetable. The time to begin grieving — and healing — is now.

When the shock wears off, we begin
to experience the full impact and pain
of facing the finality of our loss.
Judy Tatelbaum

Let us define the stages of grieving
as feelings or emotions or a state of
mind, and know that they come
and go like the tide.
Genevieve Davis Ginsburg

Grief does not neatly end when
others may think it should.
Kathlyn S. Baldwin

In the grieving process, many early steps
will fail, but they still must be taken
in order to have some experience
upon which to build.
Harriet Sarnoff Schiff

Each of us deals with grief in a different
way and on a different timetable.
Zig Ziglar

There is no grief which time
does not lessen and soften.

Cicero

Your grieving, your timing and your progress are uniquely yours, and that's the way it should be.

James E. Miller

Grief is different for everyone.
There are no recipes for grief.
Helen Fitzgerald

Of all the challenges you face in working
through grief, none is more demanding
than the endurance it requires.
Bob Deits

Each of us will experience grief
in our own way.
Judy Tatelbaum

The greater the loss,
the longer your
recovery will be.

Alla Renée Bozarth

Time will aid in recovery, but it is time
that needs to be used well….
Time spent frantically running
from grief will not help.

Helen Fitzgerald

There is wisdom in the traditional one
year of mourning, which enables the
bereaved to take at least some of the time
necessary to experience and complete
the grieving process.

Judy Tatelbaum

Many bereaved people call the second
year their lonely year.

Bob Deits

Don't expect grief to be logical.
Zig Ziglar

Grief can come without warning.
Elizabeth Jennings

Grief teaches the steadiest minds
to waver.

Sophocles

The mourning period is really a time
of convalescence.

Judy Tatelbaum

Be patient with yourself; grief takes time. You will want to rush the process, but it moves at its own pace.
Catherine M. Sanders

People are often fooled into thinking that grief moves out steadily, with every day being a little better. It doesn't work that way.
Genevieve Davis Ginsburg

In dealing with grief, there are no set rules, no right or wrong feelings.
Harriet Sarnoff Schiff

The lowest ebb is the turn of the tide.
Henry Wadsworth Longfellow

Weeping may endure for a night,
but joy cometh in the morning.
Psalm 30:5

Sadness flies away on the wings of time.

Jean de la Fontaine

Bereavement has a
turning point, but it is
hard to determine
where it is and when
we've reached it.

Catherine M. Sanders

Sadness flies on the wings of morning, and out of the darkness comes the light.

Jean Giraudoux

God gives quietness at last.

John Greenleaf Whittier

Remember one important thing about your grief: you will feel better eventually.

Catherine M. Sanders

6

Healthy Grieving

After every tragedy, there comes a time for healing. Healing is either helped or hindered by the ways in which we manage our feelings of grief. If we bottle up emotions, if we deny reality, if we fail to attend to our own needs, then we delay healing. But if we seek out supportive friends and family, if we express the depth of our sorrow, if we actively seek to move ourselves into and through the grieving process, we hasten the return to normalcy.

On the pages that follow, we consider healthy ways of facing and working through grief. If you've experienced a significant loss, and if you're sincerely ready for the healing to begin, please take the following ideas to heart.

The only feelings that do not heal are the ones you hide.

Henri Nouwen

Acknowledge that you are grieving and allow the grief to run its full course in your life.

Zig Ziglar

The time to grieve is now.

Ellen Sue Stern

Suppressed grief
suffocates.

Ovid

Telling your story will be the most
important thing you will do as a
mourner, because in the very act
of telling it, you are putting your
life back together.

Glen W. Davidson

Share your thoughts and emotions
with people who care and understand
your grief.

Kathlyn S. Baldwin

People who have suffered understand
suffering and therefore extend
their hands.

Patti Smith

Seek out persons whom you trust…
    talk to them about your loss
        and its meaning.
                        Alla Renée Bozarth

When anyone wants you to hold
    your grief in check, remember what
they are seeking is their own comfort.
                        Bob Deits

However you choose to express
        yourself, know that you are
    encouraging your own healing by
doing what you do. You are finding
        ways to accept, bit by bit, the
    reality of what it all means.
                        James E. Miller

Crying is one of the healthiest things you can do.

Bob Deits

I almost never cry, but lately
I cry all the time, and I think it helps.

Lance Armstrong

Your grief is a symbol of the quality of the relationship you had with the person who died.

Bob Deits

Ride out the low
periods knowing that
they are getting shorter
all the time.

Catherine M. Sanders

There is help for your grief!
Most of it is at the end of your arm;
you have to do it yourself.
Stanley P. Cornils

There is one person who can take care
of you better than anyone,
and that is you.
James E. Miller

If you are willing to work your way
through, there can be an end to
the sorrow and hopelessness.
Stanley P. Cornils

Successful grief work
depends on accepting
the loss and changes
that will have to take
place in our lives.

Catherine M. Sanders

Facing reality is an essential part
of grieving.

Ellen Sue Stern

Mourners must come to realize that
time cannot be turned back. The change
that has occurred with the death of a
loved one is irreversible.

Glen W. Davidson

Grief drives men into habits of serious reflection, sharpens the understanding and softens the heart.

John Adams

The hope of grief lies in our ability to grow. Many lessons present themselves throughout the grieving process.

Catherine M. Sanders

You have a choice in
how you respond
to your loss.

James E. Miller

Out of suffering have emerged
the strongest souls; the most massive
characters are seared with scars.
E. H. Chapin

The soul would have no rainbow
had the eyes no tears.
John Vance Cheney

Happiness is beneficial for the body,
but it is grief that develops the
powers of the mind.
Marcel Proust

I shall be richer all my life for this sorrow.

Elisabeth Kübler-Ross

7

Living Again

The experience of profound grief is, by its very nature, transformational. The grieving process leaves the mourner forever changed.

If you have suffered a life-changing loss of any kind, your world has been put on hold. In the early days of your grief, you feel shocked. As that shock wears off, you may feel bitter or despondent. But eventually, as you face your sorrow and share your feelings with others, you'll begin to accept the reality of your new circumstances. With this acceptance comes healing.

For every tragedy, there is a time to weep and a time to heal. Now, perhaps, is your time to heal. As that healing takes place, you will become a different person, transformed by the knowledge that a new life does indeed exist on the other side of despair. Armed with that knowledge, you can share your wisdom and, in doing so, lighten the burdens of others.

Mourning has its necessities, but
there comes a time when
it should be done with.

John Hinton

Sorrow is a fruit; God does not
make it grow on limbs too weak
to bear it.

Victor Hugo

In the aftermath of our tears,
hope rises to fill the part of us
that has been cleansed
by the pain.

Zig Ziglar

Earth has no sorrow that heaven cannot heal.

Thomas More

Faith is a bridge across
the gulf of death.
Edward Young

Sometimes when someone has died,
we say, "I feel like they're still here."
That's because they are.
Marianne Williamson

The ultimate goal of grief work
is to be able to remember
without emotional pain.
Elisabeth Kübler-Ross

Love is timeless…
   death does not separate the lover
      from the beloved.
            Kahlil Gibran

Treasure the memories of past
   misfortunes; they constitute
     our bank of fortitude.
            Eric Hoffer

You don't ever completely "get over"
  profound grief. You incorporate the
    grief into your life, and you
      choose to live again.
            Bob Powers

I walked a mile with sorrow,
  and ne'er a word said she;
But, oh, the things I learned from her
 When sorrow walked with me.
     Robert Browning

Your time of loss can become a time
   of discovery.
     James E. Miller

Every grief encounter is
  an opportunity to grow.
     Charlie Walton

That which does not destroy me
makes me stronger.

Nietzsche

You will find your grief producing
growth — a growth that is almost
indiscernible at first.

Carol Stauda

Tomorrow will be a new day.
When God sends the dawn,
He sends it for all.

Cervantes

The way out of grief is through it.

Bob Deits

Each of us can be a creative survivor.

Judy Tatelbaum

Choosing to live again means taking
charge of your grief.
Bob Deits

The only way out is ahead, and our
choice is whether we shall cringe
from it or affirm it.
Rollo May

Loss can launch the survivor
into a new life.
Judy Tatelbaum

Grieving is a process rather than
a series of uphill steps, and gains
are most often realized in retrospect.
Genevieve Davis Ginsburg

We come out of grief as deeper
persons because we have been down
in the depths of despair.
Granger Westberg

Most of us — to our own
amazement — mobilize our
inner resources and grow even
stronger for having coped.
Genevieve Davis Ginsburg

In a sense, mourning is a time of new
mastery over ourselves and our lives.
Judy Tatelbaum

Perhaps the most important message
is that if you allow yourself to sink,
there will have been a double tragedy.
It is a tragedy you can avert.
Harriet Sarnoff Schiff

What finally heals us?
When we actively move through
the phases of grief and work toward
restoring healthy perspective.
Catherine M. Sanders

When God shuts a door, He opens a window.

John Ruskin

Eventually, we realize a sense of release. Instead of being obsessed with memories of the deceased, mourners begin to give attention to the challenges and opportunities for living.

Glen W. Davidson

Success is finishing what God gave you to do.

Harold Cook

A sign of recovery is renewed energy.

Glen W. Davidson

Acceptance is
the net result of a
healthy grief process.

Harriet Sarnoff Schiff

Relying on God has to begin
  over again every day as if nothing
    had yet been done.

C. S. Lewis

Be patient toward all that is
  unresolved in your heart and try
  to love the questions themselves.

Rainer Rilke

In three words I can sum up
  everything I've learned about life:
    It Goes On.

Robert Frost

The spiritual seeker says, "My life is a classroom. I am learning something important, even from this."

Mary Hayes-Grieco

Joy is the serious business of heaven.

C. S. Lewis

It's okay
to live again.
Bob Deits

Be hopeful!
For tomorrow has never happened before.
Robert Schuller

Appendix: Things You Can Do

Marshalling Your Resources

As you work through your grief, you will find it helpful to utilize all the resources that are available to you. It is your responsibility to seek out help when you need it. Of course, you should lean upon the love, help, and support of family and friends. Other important resources include:

1. Your local place of worship.
2. Various local counseling services including, but not limited to, psychologists, counselors, pastoral counselors, and community mental health facilities.
3. Group counseling programs which may deal with your specific loss. Talking with others who have experienced a loss similar to yours will be extremely helpful.
4. Your personal physician.
5. The local bookstore or library which contains specific reading material about your grief and about your particular loss.

Holidays and Anniversaries

Holidays, anniversaries, and birthdays are times when memories come flooding back. During these times, you may find yourself dreading the prospect of another "sad day." As these days approach, consider the following:

1. Don't try to gloss over or ignore important dates. Instead, prepare yourself for the upcoming events by talking about your feelings with family, trusted friends, or counselors.

2. Don't be upset if a particular holiday or anniversary is a sad occasion. And don't for a single minute believe that all future holidays will be lonely. Instead, remind yourself that things will gradually improve with time.

3. If you know a difficult day is looming on the horizon, take the initiative to be with family or friends. Make it your responsibility to contact others; don't wait for them to contact you.

4. Don't feel guilty if you enjoy the holiday or anniversary. Your ability to laugh — even if that laughter is mixed with tears — is a sign that healing has begun.

Sleep

Periods of grief often result in disturbed sleep or in a total lack of sleep. In such cases, consider the following:

1. Reduce your intake of caffeine or, if needed, eliminate caffeine entirely from your diet. The residual effects of too much coffee or too many soft drinks may be contributing to your sleeplessness.
2. At least one hour before bedtime, begin the process of preparing for sleep by putting yourself into a calmer state. Don't watch television programs that might upset you or "get your juices flowing." Instead, engage in quieter pursuits (such as reading) in order to ready yourself for a good night's sleep. Then, in a more peaceful state, you can fall asleep more easily.
3. If you can't fall asleep quickly, don't lie in bed and worry about the fact that you are not sleeping. Instead, get up, pick up a book, and read until you feel tired. Then go back to bed. Your bed should be a place for sleeping, not a place for worrying.

4. Establish regular sleep patterns by getting up at the same time every day. Even if you don't fall asleep until a very late hour, force yourself out of bed at the same time each morning. This practice will, within a few weeks, help you establish a more normal pattern of sleep.

5. Troubles and worries are always magnified during the nighttime hours. If you are too worried about a particular topic to fall asleep, do not lie in bed and obsess over the problem. Instead, get up, take pencil and paper, and write down your worries along with an action plan to solve them.

6. Engage in sensible physical exercise on a regular basis.

7. If you drink alcohol, drink in moderation. Too much alcohol interrupts normal sleep.

8. If you, or someone close to you, feels that your lack of sleep is posing a hazard to your physical or emotional well-being, consult your physician.

9. Remember the words of Victor Hugo: "Have courage for all the great sorrows of life and patience for the small ones. And when you have finished your daily task, go to sleep. God is awake."

Grief Versus Depression

Grief is a natural response to any significant loss. Grief runs its course and gradually abates over time. Depression, on the other hand, is a physical and emotional condition that is, in almost all cases, treatable by counseling, medication, or both. Left untreated, depression is extremely dangerous to your physical health and to your emotional well-being.

If you have recently experienced a traumatic loss, grief is unavoidable. But if you, or someone close to you, fears that your grief may have evolved into clinical depression, it's time to seek professional help. Consider the following:

1. If you have persistent urges toward self-destructive behavior, or if you feel as though you have lost the will to live, consult a professional counselor or physician immediately.
2. If someone you trust urges you to seek counseling, schedule a session with a professionally trained counselor to evaluate your condition.

3. If you experience persistent and prolonged changes in sleep patterns, or if you experience a significant change in weight (either gain or loss), consult your physician.

4. If you are plagued by consistent, prolonged, severe feelings of hopelessness or apathy, consult a physician or professional counselor.

In summary, depression is a serious but treatable condition. If you suspect that depression may have a grip on you or someone you love, seek professional guidance without delay. As the old saying goes: "Better safe than sorry."

Putting Your Feelings on Paper

You may find it helpful to write down your feelings and memories. Consider the following:

1. You may wish to begin keeping a journal of your thoughts and experiences. As you commit your emotions to paper, you are "working through" your sorrow in a tangible way. Furthermore, you can use your journal as a history of your experiences, thus allowing yourself to gauge the healing that is taking place in your life.
2. You may wish to create a scrapbook of pictures and other reminders of the deceased. The scrapbook is not only a tribute your loved one, it is also a way of processing your grief.
3. You may wish to compose a letter to the deceased expressing your feelings of love, anger, fear, loss and hope. This letter may also contain words that you wish you had spoken to the deceased, but didn't.

Finding New Meaning for Living

Perhaps your loss has turned your world upside down. Perhaps everything in your life has been changed forever. Perhaps your relationships and your responsibilities have been permanently altered. If so, you may come face-to-face with the daunting task of finding a new purpose for living.

Your suffering carries with it great potential: the potential for intense personal growth and the potential to help others. As you begin to reorganize your life, always be watchful for ways to use your suffering for the betterment of others. Lend your experienced hand to help fellow travelers, knowing that the course of your healing will depend upon how quickly you discover new people to help and new reasons to live.

As you move through and beyond your grief, be mindful of this fact: As a wounded survivor, you will have countless opportunities to serve others. And by serving others, you will bring meaning to the suffering you've endured.

Sources

Adams, John 83

Alfred, Lord Tennyson 36

Armstrong, Lance 78

Baldwin, Kathlyn S. 26, 32, 35, 56, 76

Bozarth, Alla Renée 34, 39, 52, 60, 77

Brothers, Joyce 20

Browning, Robert 92

Byron, Lord 13

Cervantes 93

Chapin, E. H. 85

Cheney, John Vance 85

Cicero 57

Cook, Harold 100

Cornils, Stanley P. 39, 80

Crabbe, George 24

Davidson, Glen W. 36, 37, 38, 42, 76, 82, 100

Deits, Bob 25, 33, 50, 51, 59, 61, 77, 78, 94, 96, 105

Fitzgerald, Helen 30, 38, 43, 59, 61

Fontaine, Jean la de 66

Frost, Robert 102

Gibran, Kahlil 91

Ginsburg, Genevieve Davis 20, 42, 44, 56, 64, 97

Giraudoux, Jean 68

Hayes, Helen 28

Hayes-Grieco, Mary 103

Hinton, John 88

Hoffer, Eric 91

Hugo, Victor 88

Jennings, Elizabeth 62

Kübler-Ross, Elisabeth 86, 90

Kushner, Harold S. 50

Lewis, C. S. 27, 47, 102, 104

Longfellow, Henry Wadsworth 65

May, Rollo 96

Miller, James E. 22, 28, 58, 77, 80, 84, 92

Moore, James W. 24

More, Thomas 89

Nathan, Robert 30

Nietzsche 93

Nouwen, Henri 72

Oates, Wayne 24, 44, 48, 49

Ovid 34, 75

Powers, Bob 91

Proust, Marcel 85

Publilius Syrus 15

Rilke, Rainer 102

Ruskin, John 99

Saint-Exupéry, Antoine de 30

Sanders, Catherine M. 20, 21, 22, 27, 42, 48, 64, 67, 70, 79, 81, 83, 98

Schiff, Harriet Sarnoff 26, 36, 37, 40, 43, 57, 64, 98, 101

Schuller, Robert 106

Shakespeare, William 35

Smith, Patti 76

Sophocles 63

Stauda, Carol 93

Staudacher, Carol 37, 43

Stern, Ellen Sue 45, 74, 82

Tatelbaum, Judy 27, 44, 46, 48, 50, 56, 59, 61, 63, 95, 96, 98

Voltaire 35

Walton, Charlie 21, 29, 92

Webster, Noah 23

Westberg, Granger 22, 25, 97

Williamson, Marianne 90

Whittier, John Greenleaf 69

Young, Edward 90

Ziglar, Zig 21, 26, 32, 57, 62, 73, 88

About the Author

Criswell Freeman is a Doctor of Clinical Psychology living in Nashville, Tennessee. In addition to this text, Dr. Freeman is also the author of many other books including his bestselling self help book *When Life Throws You a Curveball, Hit It.*

About
DELANEY STREET PRESS

DELANEY STREET PRESS publishes books designed to inspire and entertain readers of all ages. DELANEY STREET books are distributed by Foxglove Press. For more information, call 1-877-205-1932.